Drawing Is Fun!

DRAWING
CREEPY CRAWLIES

Gareth Stevens
Publishing

Please visit our website, www.garethstevens.com. For a free color catalog of all our high-quality books, call toll free 1-800-542-2595 or fax 1-877-542-2596.

Library of Congress Cataloging-in-Publication Data

Clunes, Rebecca.
Drawing creepy crawlies / Rebecca Clunes.
    p. cm.— (Drawing is fun)
Includes index.
ISBN 978-1-4339-5940-0 (pbk.)
ISBN 978-1-4339-5941-7 (6-pack)
ISBN 978-1-4339-5938-7 (library binding)
1. Insects in art—Juvenile literature. 2. Invertebrates in art—Juvenile literature. 3. Drawing—Technique—Juvenile literature. I. Title.
NC783.C58 2011
743.6—dc22

2010052605

First Edition

Published in 2012 by
Gareth Stevens Publishing
111 East 14th Street, Suite 349
New York, NY 10003

Copyright © 2012 Arcturus Publishing

Cartoon illustrations: Dynamo Limited
Text: Rebecca Clunes and Dynamo Limited
Editors: Anna Brett, Kate Overy, and Joe Harris
Design: Tokiko Morishima
Cover design: Tokiko Morishima

Picture credits: All images supplied by Shutterstock.

Printed in China

CPSIA compliance information: Batch # AS11GS: For further information contact Gareth Stevens, New York, New York at 1-800-542-2595.

SL001842US

Contents

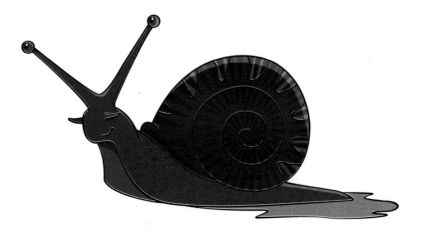

Scorpion

This scorpion's tail has a sting at the end.

She curls her tail up over her back.

She has big claws for grabbing hold of her food.

She has eight legs.

FUN FACTS ● FUN FACTS ● FUN FACTS ● FUN FACTS ● FUN FACTS

Mother scorpions look after their babies. They climb on her back and get a ride!

1. This shape makes the body and the tail.

2. Add snapping claws at the front.

3. Don't forget the legs on either side of the body.

4. Color your scorpion, but make sure that you don't get stung by that tail!

Praying mantis

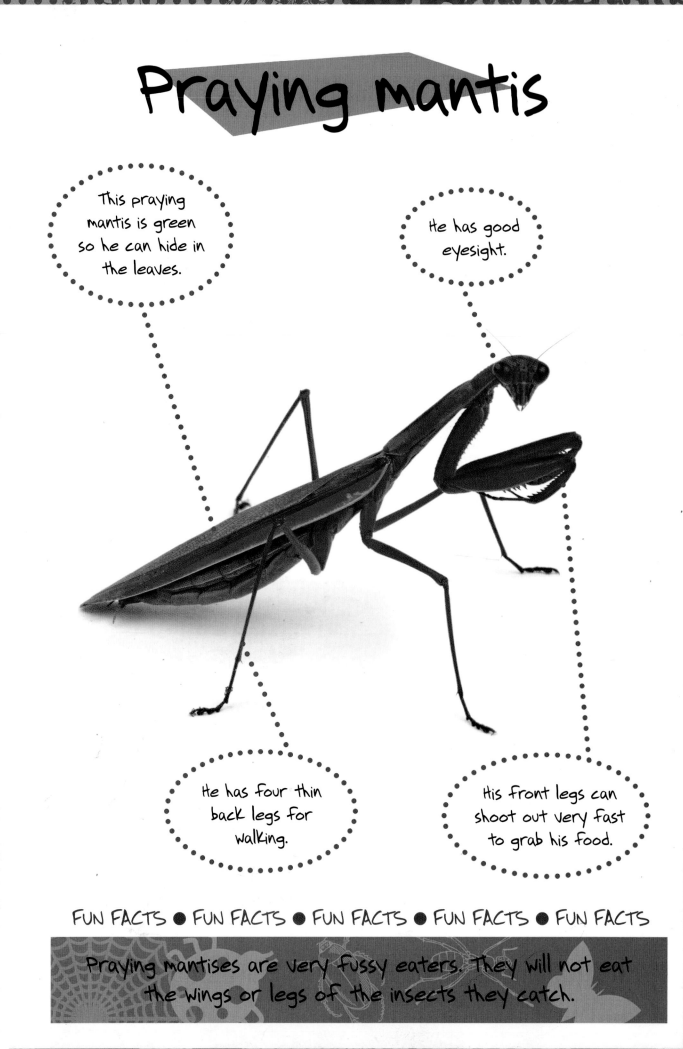

This praying mantis is green so he can hide in the leaves.

He has good eyesight.

He has four thin back legs for walking.

His front legs can shoot out very fast to grab his food.

FUN FACTS ● FUN FACTS ● FUN FACTS ● FUN FACTS ● FUN FACTS

Praying mantises are very fussy eaters. They will not eat the wings or legs of the insects they catch.

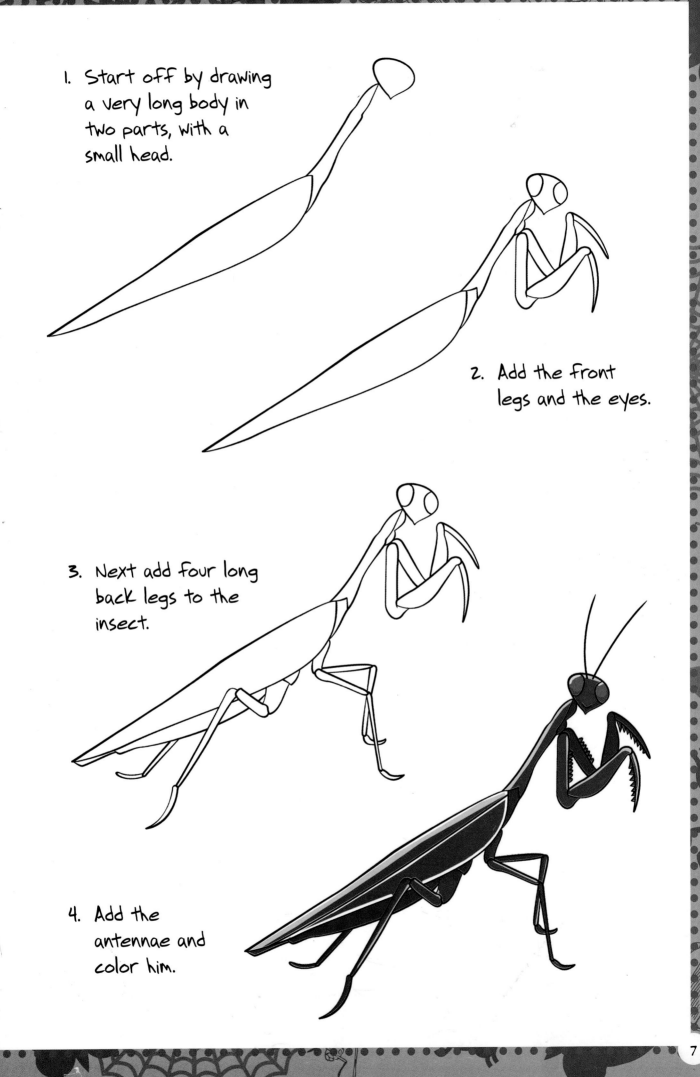

1. Start off by drawing a very long body in two parts, with a small head.

2. Add the front legs and the eyes.

3. Next add four long back legs to the insect.

4. Add the antennae and color him.

Fly

This fly has a hairy body.

She has two wings and is very good at flying.

She has big eyes to see all around her.

She tastes her food through her feet.

FUN FACTS ● FUN FACTS ● FUN FACTS ● FUN FACTS ● FUN FACTS

Flies eat rotting meat and fruit.

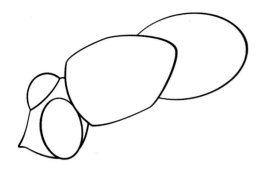

1. Start with this shape.

2. Add the large wings.

3. The thin legs are next.

4. Color her, making the wings light blue. Don't forget to add tiny hairs to the body.

Caterpillar

This caterpillar eats leaves. He grows very fast.

When he gets too big for his old skin, he will wriggle out of it. There is a new, bigger skin underneath.

He can hang from a silk thread which comes out of his mouth.

He has a long, round body and lots of legs.

FUN FACTS ● FUN FACTS ● FUN FACTS ● FUN FACTS ● FUN FACTS

Caterpillars hatch out of eggs. Later they will turn into butterflies or moths.

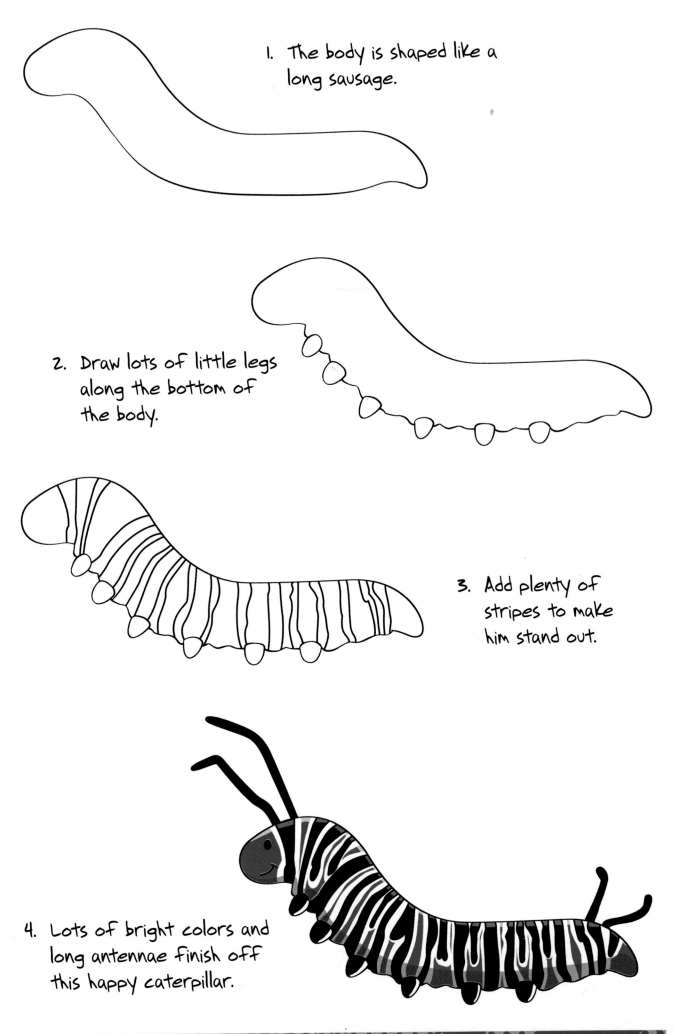

1. The body is shaped like a long sausage.

2. Draw lots of little legs along the bottom of the body.

3. Add plenty of stripes to make him stand out.

4. Lots of bright colors and long antennae finish off this happy caterpillar.

Snail

This snail's eyes are at the top of her two biggest feelers.

She can tuck her body inside her shell if she is in danger.

The shorter feelers are used for smelling.

She has no legs and moves slowly on her soft body.

FUN FACTS ● FUN FACTS ● FUN FACTS ● FUN FACTS ● FUN FACTS

Snails leave a trail of slime behind them. The slime makes it easier for them to move.

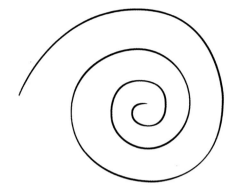

1. Start with a simple spiral.

2. Draw in a slug-shaped body.

3. Add her feelers and her eyes.

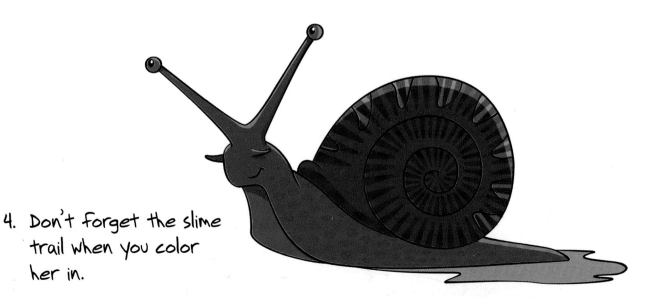

4. Don't forget the slime trail when you color her in.

Grasshopper

This grasshopper has long back legs that are good for jumping.

He can fly, but not very well.

He has four shorter legs for walking.

He is the same color as the leaves he lives on.

FUN FACTS ● FUN FACTS ● FUN FACTS ● FUN FACTS ● FUN FACTS

Male grasshoppers make music by rubbing their legs against their wings.

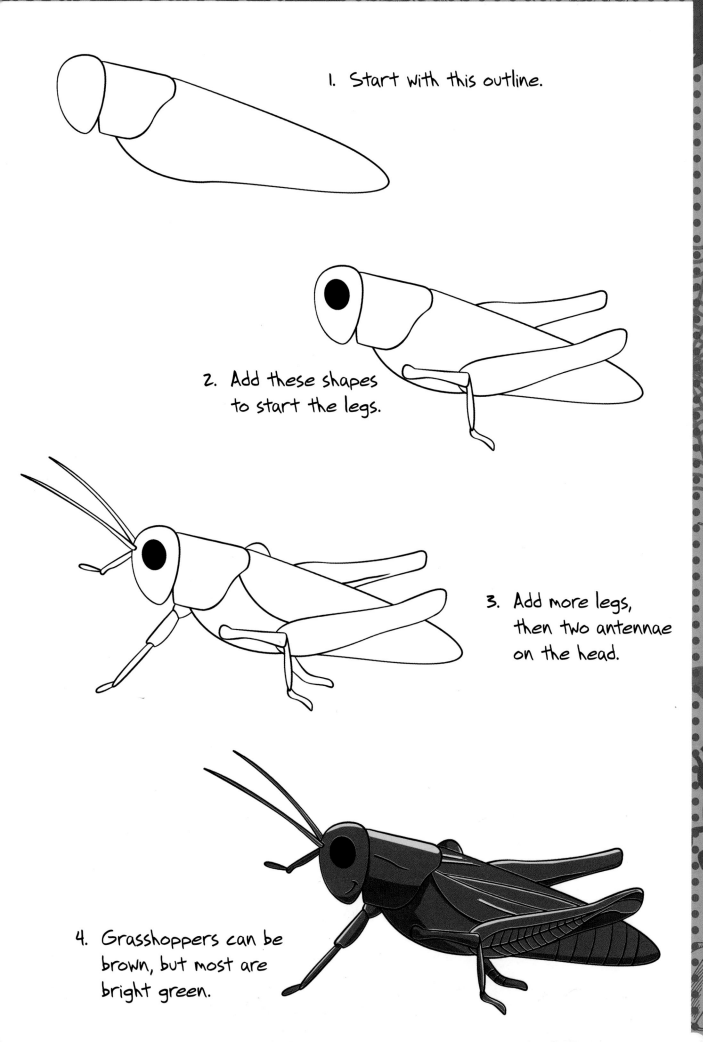

1. Start with this outline.

2. Add these shapes to start the legs.

3. Add more legs, then two antennae on the head.

4. Grasshoppers can be brown, but most are bright green.

Butterfly

This butterfly is a beautiful blue color.

Her mouth is like a straw. She drinks nectar from flowers.

She flies in the day, not at night.

She has a long, thin, smooth body.

FUN FACTS ● FUN FACTS ● FUN FACTS ● FUN FACTS ● FUN FACTS

One type of butterfly travels from Canada to Mexico, a journey of over 2,000 miles (around 3,200 kilometers).

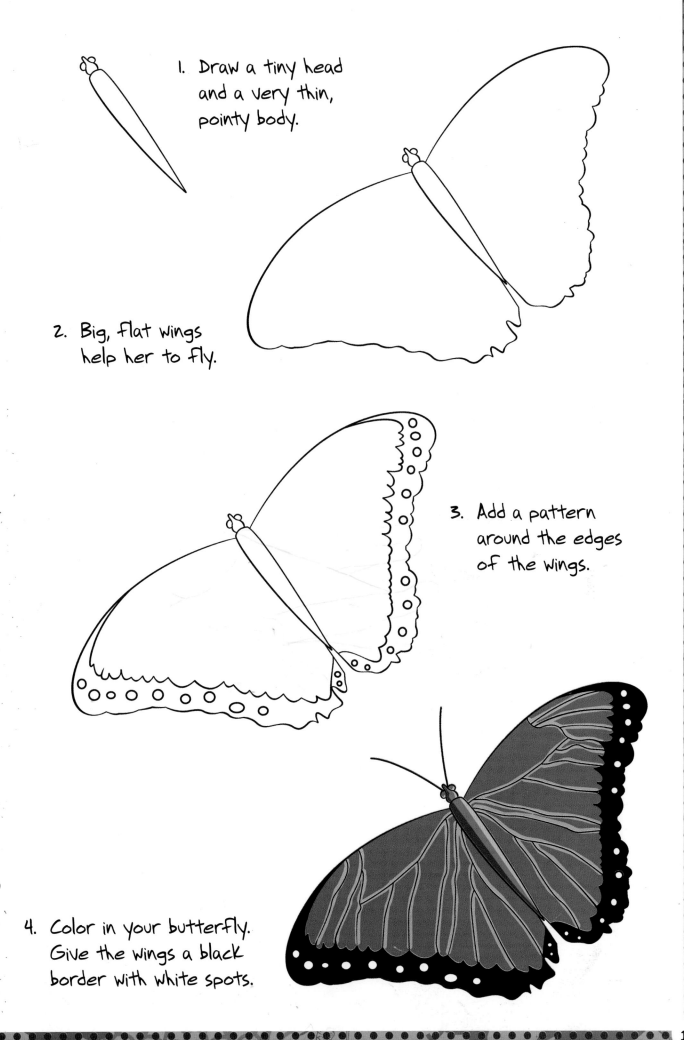

1. Draw a tiny head and a very thin, pointy body.

2. Big, flat wings help her to fly.

3. Add a pattern around the edges of the wings.

4. Color in your butterfly. Give the wings a black border with white spots.

Ladybug

This ladybug is red with seven black spots.

Her wings are under her hard back.

She eats small, soft insects such as aphids.

She has six legs.

FUN FACTS ● FUN FACTS ● FUN FACTS ● FUN FACTS ● FUN FACTS

In the fall, ladybugs gather together in a safe, sheltered spot. They sleep through the winter.

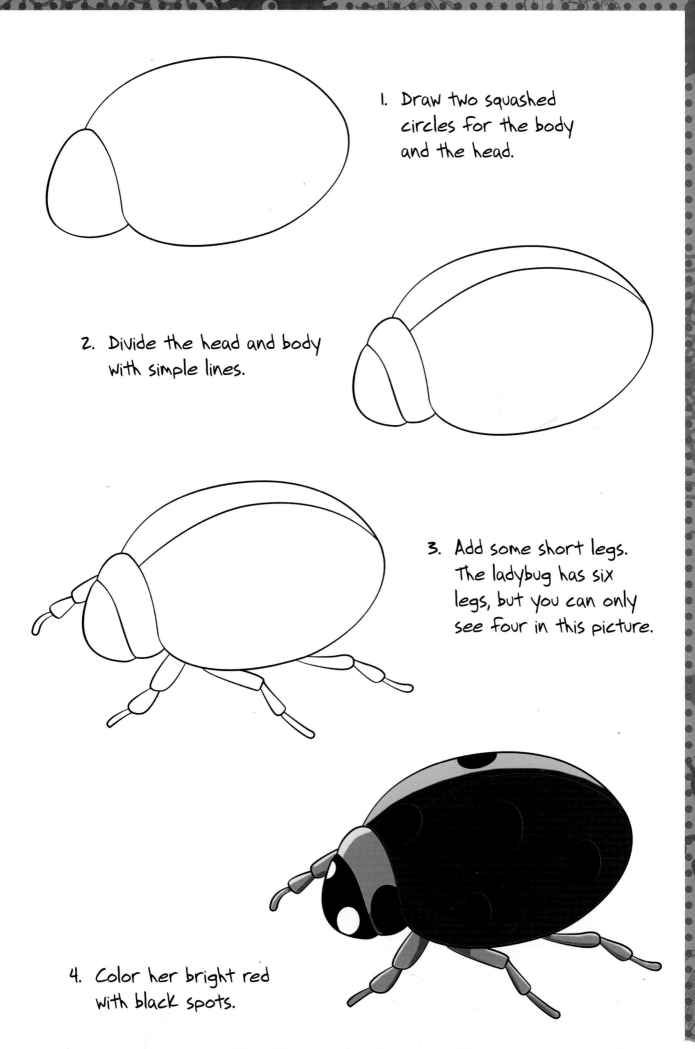

1. Draw two squashed circles for the body and the head.

2. Divide the head and body with simple lines.

3. Add some short legs. The ladybug has six legs, but you can only see four in this picture.

4. Color her bright red with black spots.

Dragonfly

This dragonfly has four wings. She's a very good flier.

She has a brightly colored body.

She has huge eyes.

She catches her food with her front two legs.

FUN FACTS ● FUN FACTS ● FUN FACTS ● FUN FACTS ● FUN FACTS

Young dragonflies live underwater for several years. Only adults have wings and can fly.

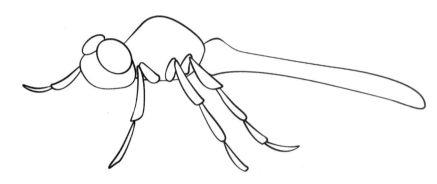

1. Draw these shapes to make the head and body.

2. Add some legs. Dragonflies have six legs, but you can only see four in this picture.

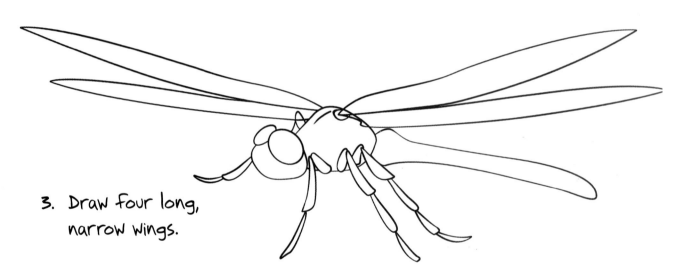

3. Draw four long, narrow wings.

4. Color the wings pale blue to make them look see-through.

Centipede

She eats insects, spiders, and worms. Her bite is poisonous.

Her body has lots of parts. Each part has two legs.

This centipede has a hard body and lots of legs.

Her back legs are longer than her front legs.

FUN FACTS ● FUN FACTS ● FUN FACTS ● FUN FACTS ● FUN FACTS

Some centipedes are 10 inches (25 cm) long, and big enough to eat mice and birds.

1. Draw a long, curvy sausage shape with a circle at the top.

2. Add these lines to show how her body has lots of parts.

3. Add lots and lots of legs!

4. Don't forget to add the antennae on her head.

Stag beetle

This stag beetle has a hard body.

He has big jaws that he uses to fight other males.

Female stag beetles are smaller than males. They do not have big jaws.

He has wings. They are hidden under here.

FUN FACTS ● FUN FACTS ● FUN FACTS ● FUN FACTS ● FUN FACTS

Stag beetles lay their eggs in old wood. Young beetles live in the wood or under the ground for several years.

1. Two squashed circles and one long oval make the head and body.

2. Add his huge jaws at the front.

3. Draw legs that get thinner at the ends.

4. Finish off by coloring him brown and black.

Moth

This moth has brown wings so that he can hide on trees during the day.

His antennae pick up smells so he can find food or female moths.

When he rests his wings open flat.

He has stripes on his body.

FUN FACTS • FUN FACTS • FUN FACTS • FUN FACTS • FUN FACTS

Most moths fly at night. They can get confused by electric lights and fly close to them.

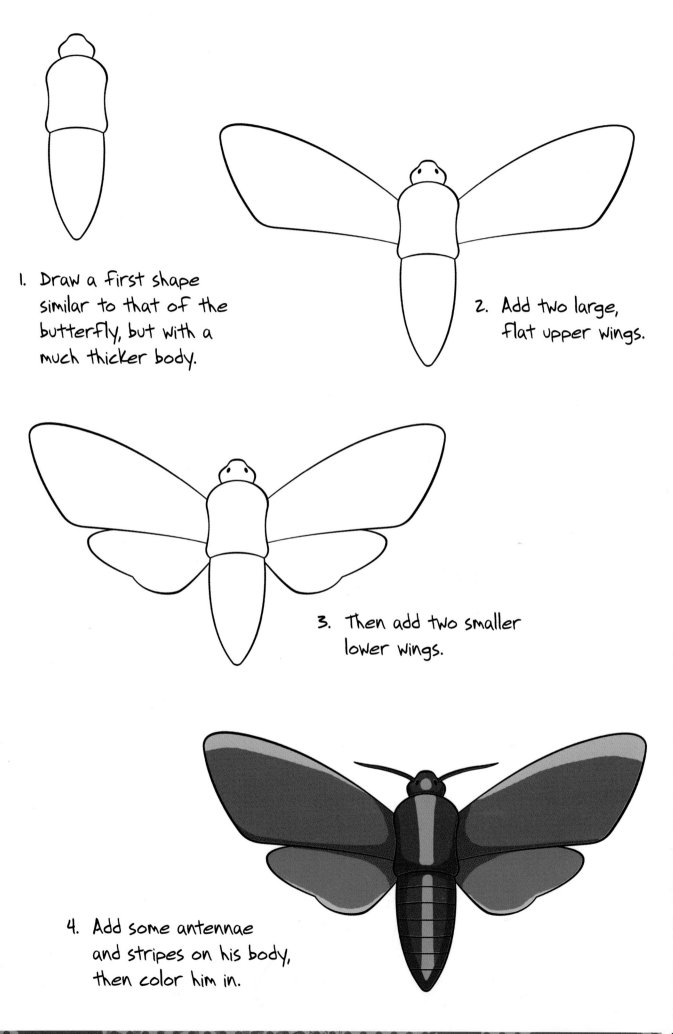

1. Draw a first shape similar to that of the butterfly, but with a much thicker body.

2. Add two large, flat upper wings.

3. Then add two smaller lower wings.

4. Add some antennae and stripes on his body, then color him in.

Ant

This ant has six legs. Her body has four parts.

Ants are small, about half an inch (1 cm) long.

Her antennae have a bend in the middle of them.

Ants are very strong for their size.

FUN FACTS ● FUN FACTS ● FUN FACTS ● FUN FACTS ● FUN FACTS

Ants live in big groups. Each group has one queen and lots of workers. The workers gather the food and look after the nest.

1. These shapes make up the body and head.

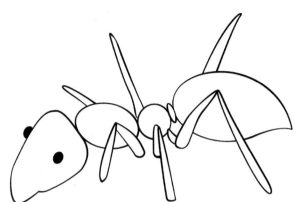

2. Add two eyes to the head and start the six legs.

3. Finish the legs and you are nearly done.

4. Add the antennae and tiny hairs on the legs, then color her in.

Bumblebee

She is brightly colored with black and yellow stripes

She has a sting at the end of her body.

This bumblebee lives with lots of other bees in a nest under the ground.

Her body is covered in hair to keep her warm.

FUN FACTS ● FUN FACTS ● FUN FACTS ● FUN FACTS ● FUN FACTS

Bees move their wings very fast. Their wings make a buzzing noise when they fly.

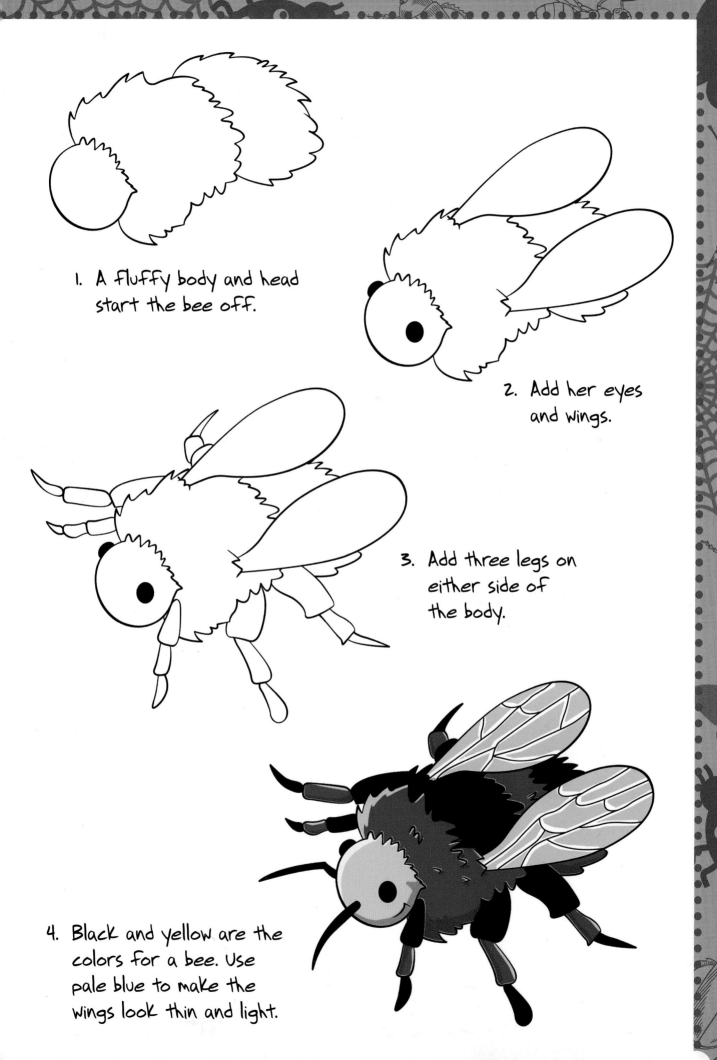

1. A fluffy body and head start the bee off.

2. Add her eyes and wings.

3. Add three legs on either side of the body.

4. Black and yellow are the colors for a bee. Use pale blue to make the wings look thin and light.

Glossary

antennae the feelers on top of an insect's head, used for smelling and touching

aphid a tiny insect that lives on plants

confused finding something difficult to understand

female an animal that could become a mother

jaw the outer part of an insect's mouth

journey to travel from one place to another

male an animal that could become a father

nectar a sweet liquid made by plants

poisonous contains a liquid that kills or injures an animal

sheltered safe, warm, and dry

silk a strong thread made by an insect

slime thick, slippery liquid

sting a sharp point on an animal's body that can be used to hurt another animal

Further Reading

Bull, Peter. *Quick Draw Creepy-Crawlies*. Kingfisher, 2008.

Fisher, Diana. *Insects: Step-by-Step Instructions for 26 Creepy Crawlies.* Walter Foster, 2007.

Masiello, Ralph. *Bug Drawing Book*. Charlesbridge Publishing, 2004.

Index

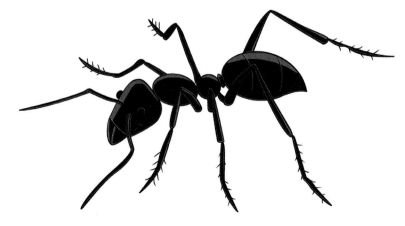